Wall Street—How It Works

The Basic Investor's Library

Chelsea House Publishers

Wall Street— How It Works

JEFFREY B. LITTLE

Paul A. Samuelson
Senior Editorial Consultant

CHELSEA HOUSE PUBLISHERS   New York   Philadelphia

Editor-in-Chief   Nancy Toff
Executive Editor   Remmel T. Nunn
Managing Editor   Karyn Gullen Browne
Copy Chief   Juliann Barbato
Picture Editor   Adrian G. Allen
Art Director   Giannella Garrett
Manufacturing Manager   Gerald Levine

Staff for   WALL STREET—HOW IT WORKS
Senior Editor   Marjorie P. K. Weiser
Associate Editor   Andrea E. Reynolds
Copyeditors   Sean Dolan, Ellen Scordato
Associate Picture Editor   Juliette Dickstein
Senior Designer   Laurie Jewell
Designer   Barbara Bachman
Production Coordinator   Laura McCormick

Creative Director   Harold Steinberg

Contributing Editor   Robert W. Wrubel
Consulting Editor   Shawn Patrick Burke

5   7   9   8   6   4

Library of Congress Cataloging-in-Publication Data

Little, Jeffrey B.
  Wall Street—how it works.

  (The Basic investor's library)
  Bibliography: p.
  Includes index.

  1. Investments—United States—Juvenile literature.
2. Stocks—United States—Juvenile literature.
3. Stock-exchange—United States—Juvenile literature.
4. Wall Street—Juvenile literature.   [1. Investments.
2. Stocks. 3. Stock exchange. 4. Wall Street]

I. Samuelson, Paul Anthony, 1915–   .   II. Title.
III. Series.
HG4921.L625   1988   332.64′273   87-15139
ISBN 1-55546-621-4
      0-7910-0322-1 (pbk.)

CONTENTS

Learning the Tools of Investing

PAUL A. SAMUELSON

When asked why the great financial house of Morgan had been so successful, J. Pierpont Morgan replied, "Do you suppose that's because we take money seriously?"

Managing our personal finances is a serious business, and something we all must learn to do. We begin life dependent on someone else's income and capital. But after we become independent, it is a remorseless fact of nature that we must not only support ourselves for the present but must also start saving money for retirement. The best theory of saving that economists have is built upon this model of *life-cycle saving*: You must provide in the long years of prime working life for what modern medicine has lengthened to, potentially, decades of retirement. This life-cycle model won a 1985 Nobel Prize for my MIT colleague Franco Modigliani, and it points up the need to learn the rudiments of personal finance.

Learning to acquire wealth, however, is only part of the story. We must also learn to avoid losing what we have acquired. There is an old saying that "life insurance is *sold*, not bought." The same goes for stocks and bonds. In each case, the broker is guaranteed a profit, whether or not the customer benefits from the transaction. Knowledge is the customer's only true ally in the world of finance. Some gullible victims have lost their lifetime savings to unscrupulous sales promoters. One chap buys the Brooklyn Bridge. Another believes a stranger who asserts that gold will quickly double in price, with no risk of a drop in value. Such "con" (confidence) rackets get written up in the newspapers and on the police blotters every day.

6

I am concerned, however, about something less dramatic than con artists; something that is not at all illegal, but that costs ordinary citizens a thousand times more than outright embezzlement or fraud. Consider two families, neighbors who could be found in any town. They started alike. Each worked equally hard, and had about the same income. But the Smiths have to make do with half of what the Joneses have in retirement income, for one simple reason: The Joneses followed prudent practice as savers and investors, while the Smiths tried to make a killing and constantly bought and sold stocks at high commissions.

The point is, it does matter to learn how financial markets work, and how you can participate in them to your best advantage. It is important to know the difference between *common* and *preferred* stocks, between *convertible* and *zero-coupon* bonds. It is not difficult to find out what *mutual funds* are, and to understand the difference between the successful Fund A, which charges no commission, or "load," and the equally successful Fund B, which does charge the buyer such a fee.

All investing involves risk. When I was a young assistant professor, I said primly to my great Harvard teacher, Joseph Schumpeter: "We should speculate only with money we can afford to lose." He gently corrected me: "Paul, there is no such money. Besides, a speculator is merely an investor who has lost." Did Schumpeter exaggerate? Of course he did, but in the good cause of establishing the basic point of financial management: Good past performance is no guarantee of the future.

That is why *diversification* is the golden rule. "Don't put all your eggs in one basket. And watch all those baskets!" However, diversification does not mean throwing random darts at the financial pages of the newspaper to choose the best stocks in which to invest. The most diversified strategy of all would be to invest in a portfolio containing all the stocks in the comprehensive Standard & Poor's 500 Stock Index. But rather than throw random darts at the financial pages to pick out a few stocks, why not throw a large bath towel at the newspaper instead? Buy a bit of everything in proportion to its value in the larger world: Buy more General Motors than Ford, because GM is the bigger company; buy General Electric as well as GM because the auto industry is just one of many industries. That is called being an *index investor*. Index investing makes sense because 70 out of 100 investors who try to do better than the Standard & Poor's 500, the sober record shows, do worse over a 30-year period.

Do not take my word for this. The second lesson in finance is to be skeptical of what writers and other experts say, and that includes being skeptical of professors of economics. So I wish readers *Bon voyage!* on their cruise to command the fundamentals of investing. On your mainship flag, replace the motto "Nothing ventured, nothing gained" with the Latin words *Caveat emptor*—Let the buyer beware.

The New York Stock Exchange and Broad Street in 1923.

Wall Street—How It Works

Three hundred and fifty years ago, Wall Street was a dirt path running from east to west in the small Dutch settlement of New Amsterdam. Since then, that dirt path has become one of the major financial centers of the world. Yet, Wall Street, perhaps the most well known of all streets, may be one of the least understood.

People know that investing occurs on Wall Street, but many do not learn what investing is all about. They are frightened away by its apparent complexities. They may never learn of Wall Street's colorful history nor of its role in the U.S. and world economies. In the end, the way stocks are bought and sold remains a mystery to them.

Investing is indeed a challenge that requires serious study, but a stock market transaction is no more complicated than buying or selling a car or a stereo system.

This book provides a brief history of how Wall Street developed and explains what goes on there today. It discusses the different stock exchanges and describes the process of trading shares of stocks.

DEFINING WALL STREET

Wall Street is an actual street located near the southern tip of Manhattan in New York City. Specifically, it begins at South Street near the East River and extends west, ending at Broadway in front of the old Trinity Church. It is less than one mile long. But when people ask, "How does Wall Street work?" or "What happened on Wall Street this week?" it is not the street itself to which they are referring. They are talking about a whole marketplace.

The Wall Street marketplace is where merchants, customers, and agents involved in finance meet to buy and sell stocks and bonds. It is composed of all of the individual marketplaces in the United States.

Over time, the phrase "Wall Street" has become a short, convenient reference to the numerous places where stocks are traded in a two-way auction process—on the New York Stock Exchange (NYSE), the American Stock Exchange (AMEX), and the various regional stock exchanges. Also included in the reference are the nationwide network of *broker/dealers* known as the *over-the-counter market (OTC)*, brokerage firms and their employees, and a variety of individual and institutional investors. The activities of this vast marketplace are regulated by a federal government agency called the Securities and Exchange Commission (SEC).

Each person using the Wall Street marketplace has one objective: to make money. A stock buyer is trying to obtain a good return on his or her investment through dividend payments or through selling later at a higher stock price. The seller, on the other hand, may have gained or lost money by owning a stock but would like to sell the stock in order to free the money for investment somewhere else. The combined activities of buyers and sellers form an economic process that helps to create new industries and new jobs.

A HISTORY OF WALL STREET

The foot of Wall Street, 1679.

Wall Street takes its name from a wall of brush and mud that was built alongside the street's original path. Dutch settlers constructed the wall soon after establishing a trading post on the island of Manhattan, following Henry Hudson's exploration of the area in 1609. In 1626, the Dutch purchased the whole island from local Indians—for $24 and some beads—and named the post New Amsterdam. They improved their wall to keep cows in and Indians out.

The path quickly became a center of commercial and community activity because it connected the docks serving the Hudson River trade on the west end with the East River docks conducting an importing business at its other end. Leading merchants built their homes and businesses there, along with a city hall and a church.

In the 17th century, merchants had numerous interests. They bought and sold such commodities as furs, molasses, and tobacco; traded foreign and local currencies; and speculated in land. They also insured cargos. But they were not investing in stocks and bonds at this point. Stocks and bonds as we know them did not yet exist.

When the English gained control of the area in 1664, the settlement was renamed New York. Its chief economic

Founding members of the New York Stock Exchange trade securities under a buttonwood tree on Wall Street, 1792.

support remained trade and commerce throughout the 18th century. Between 1785 and 1790, New York City was the capital of the United States. In 1789, George Washington was inaugurated president on the steps of Federal Hall on Wall Street, and a few months later, the first U.S. Congress met in the same building. The first order of business was to authorize the issue of $80 million in government bonds to help pay for the recent war against England. These bonds became the first national securities available for trading. Two years later, bank stocks were added to government bonds when Alexander Hamilton, then secretary of the treasury, established the nation's first federally chartered bank, the First Bank of the United States, and offered shares of the bank's stock to the public.

Now there were securities to trade, but no organized market existed on Wall Street. The first stock exchange was established in Philadelphia in 1790. In New York, however, investors indicated their interest in available stocks and bonds directly to merchants who gathered to exchange information in Wall Street coffeehouses or by advertising in newspapers. The list of securities grew as more bank and newly formed insurance company stocks were added. It became clear that an organized market was necessary for fair and efficient trading.

By early 1792, Wall Street was enjoying its first *bull market*. Stock prices were rising because many people were eager to buy and sell the limited number of available stocks and bonds and were willing to pay higher and higher prices for them. Also, people were confident in the potential growth of the new nation and its economy. On some days, as many as 100 bank shares would be traded. Some merchants kept a small inventory of securities on hand, which they would sell over the counter like any of their other wares. (Today's *over-the-counter market* got its name from this early form of trading.)

Wall Street merchants began to schedule stock and bond auctions, as they had done for commodities. Several leading merchants, in an effort to organize the market, formed a central auction at 22 Wall Street, where securities were traded every day at noon. Customers of the newly formed "Stock Exchange Office," or their agents, left securities with the auctioneers, who received a certain amount of money, known as a *commission*, for each stock or bond sold. A customer's agent, or *broker*, would also receive a commission for shares purchased. Some people came to the Wall Street auction just to listen to the transactions. They noted the prices of the stocks and bonds, and after the auction they would offer the same securities for sale, but at reduced commission rates. Even auction members traded in this after-hours market.

Wall Street leaders, concerned with the market situation, met on March 21, 1792, to establish an improved auction market. Two months later, 24 men signed a document in which they agreed to trade securities only among themselves, maintain set commission rates, and avoid other auctions. These 24 men are considered to be the founders and original members of the New York Stock Exchange.

At first, the new brokers' organization met under a spreading buttonwood tree facing 68 Wall Street, but before long, they had expanded enough to need a building to transact business. They moved indoors when the Tontine Coffee-House—at the northwest corner of Wall and

The Old Tontine Coffee-House on Wall Street, the New York Stock Exchange's first indoor place of business, about 1800.

William Streets—was completed in 1793. Trading activity increased, and the brokers moved to larger quarters in what is now 40 Wall Street.

On March 8, 1817, the members of the organization adopted a formal constitution, creating the New York Stock and Exchange Board and a set of rules for their market. Every morning a list of all stocks to be auctioned was read to the assembled board members who would then, while seated, make bids and offers. Only members of the Board were allowed to trade; the privilege to sit at the auction cost $400. To this day, a member of the NYSE is said to own a *seat* on the Exchange.

The brokers who were unable to afford a seat on the Board or who were refused membership often found it difficult to make a living by trading securities. In poor markets, many went bankrupt.

The Board moved several times more before it took space in 1863 in a building located at the present NYSE site (11 Wall Street). Later that year, the Board adopted its current name, the New York Stock Exchange.

When gold was discovered in California in 1849, the country turned its attention to the West. The growth of the country brought new businesses and new industries. Mining stocks and railroad shares were especially popular. By 1850, Wall Street was jumping with activity. Many of the new companies were considered risky ventures. Mem-

The floor of the New York Stock Exchange, about 1907. The photograph, taken secretly through a coat sleeve, may have been the public's first actual view inside the NYSE.

bers of the Stock and Exchange Board were unwilling to trade the stocks of these companies. However, nonmember brokers eagerly traded them. Few could afford office space, so they traded in the street. By the late 1870s, the corner of William and Beaver Streets had been established as a central trading place. The corner filled daily with brokers shouting out orders to buy and sell. Because the edge of the street was defined with stones, the traders were called *curbstone brokers* and their market was known as the Curb. Even in rain and snow they conducted business there.

In the early 1890s, the Curb moved to Broad Street to gain more room. Many brokers took offices in the nearby Mills Building. There, telephone clerks took orders and shouted them down to the brokers below. But with several hundred brokers being called, more or less simultaneously, the noise made business difficult. A system of hand signaling was developed (parts of which are still used today on the AMEX) to convey stock price and volume information to the waiting brokers. Clerks would lean out of the windows of the Mills Building or balance precariously on an outside ledge, working their fingers furiously. To stand out in the crowd for their clerks, the brokers began to wear brightly colored jackets and hats. Although it looked like pandemonium, the clerks and brokers could follow everything that was going on. They knew that certain stocks were traded at specific landmarks, usually lamp posts. Action was brisk in any kind of weather.

In an effort to organize the Curb, Emanuel S. Mendels, Jr., a leading curbstone broker, organized the Curb Market Agency in 1908. The Agency developed trading rules for the market but in the end had little power to enforce them. In 1911, Mendels and his advisers drew up a formal constitution and formed the New York Curb Market Association.

Pounding his gavel first thing in the morning, a clerk announces that the New York Stock Exchange is open for business.

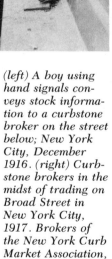

(left) A boy using hand signals conveys stock information to a curbstone broker on the street below; New York City, December 1916. (right) Curbstone brokers in the midst of trading on Broad Street in New York City, 1917. Brokers of the New York Curb Market Association, later the American Stock Exchange, conducted business outdoors until 1921.

When the curbstone brokers moved inside, one of the most colorful spectacles in American business ended. On the morning of June 27, 1921, Edward McCormick, the Curb Market's chairman, led the brokers in a march up Wall Street to their newly completed building on Trinity Place behind Trinity Church. They sang "The Star-Spangled Banner" and went inside to begin their first session on the new trading floor. Inside, each trading post was marked by a lamp post that resembled those left behind on the street.

The name of the Association changed again in 1929 to the New York Curb Exchange and then ultimately to its present name, the American Stock Exchange, in 1953.

During the 20th century, the U.S. stock market has grown tremendously. It has also been near collapse. In the 1920s, the volume of trading on the NYSE and New York Curb Market Association increased greatly, as did prices. But in October of 1929, Wall Street hit its worst point in history when investors pulled their money out of the stock market, selling millions of shares of stock in a few days. Prices plummeted, and fortunes were lost. After this disaster, the stock exchanges spent the next decade changing their systems and rebuilding.

The period between 1940 and 1960 was one of the best for the stock market. Economic growth in the country and a stronger public interest in investing in securities helped to make the stock exchanges, especially the NYSE, stable, prosperous, and powerful. During the 1970s, the AMEX and OTC gained more importance, and they competed with the NYSE to obtain company listings. This decade also saw the development of advanced computer systems, which changed the character of the exchanges as they hastened the speed of transactions and made possible far greater trading volume than ever before.

Headlines report the stock market crash of October 29, 1929, the lowest point in Wall Street's history. One newspaper called it "the most dramatic event in the financial history of America."

(continued on page 21)

A
HISTORY

17

The Dow Jones Industrial Average

I n step with the tremendous growth of the American economy, the number of businesses selling stocks on the stock market and the value of these stocks have increased more or less steadily since the market began. There have been ups and downs in the course of this

process, and these daily fluctuations are what people refer to when they say "the market went up (or down) today."

There are several standard numerical measures that describe this movement more precisely. The best known among these measures are the Dow Jones in-

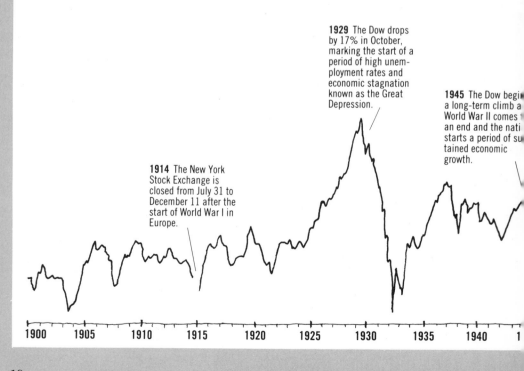

The Dow Jones Industrial Average in the 20th Century

1929 The Dow drops by 17% in October, marking the start of a period of high unemployment rates and economic stagnation known as the Great Depression.

1945 The Dow begin a long-term climb a World War II comes an end and the nati starts a period of su tained economic growth.

1914 The New York Stock Exchange is closed from July 31 to December 11 after the start of World War I in Europe.

1900 1905 1910 1915 1920 1925 1930 1935 1940 1

18 Source: "Archives of Business: Tracing the Ups and Downs of the 20th Century Through the Eyes of Wall Street," the *New York Times*, Section F, pp. 16–17, January 18, 1987.

dustrial average (Dow) and the Standard & Poor's 500–stock index (S&P 500). Each is based on a formula that uses the prices of a group of specially selected stocks. These stocks are chosen to represent different parts of the stock market as a whole. The significance of the actual Dow or S&P number is purely relative. They compare the market's position at one time to its position at another. But with these numbers, investors can track the stock market's progress from day to day. When you see graphs of the rise and fall of the stock market over time, you are looking at the change in these indexes.

The Dow is the longest-running measure of the market. Charles Dow, founder of the company that publishes the *Wall Street Journal*, devised the

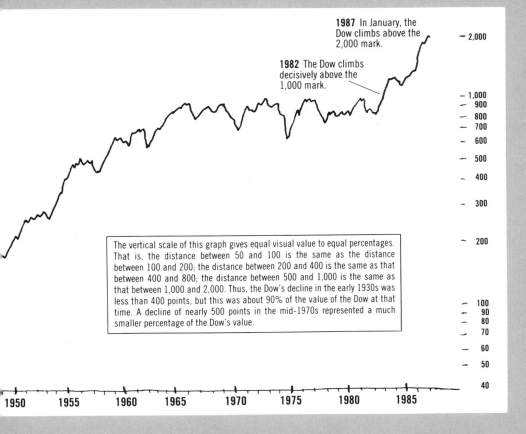

1987 In January, the Dow climbs above the 2,000 mark.

1982 The Dow climbs decisively above the 1,000 mark.

The vertical scale of this graph gives equal visual value to equal percentages. That is, the distance between 50 and 100 is the same as the distance between 100 and 200; the distance between 200 and 400 is the same as that between 400 and 800; the distance between 500 and 1,000 is the same as that between 1,000 and 2,000. Thus, the Dow's decline in the early 1930s was less than 400 points, but this was about 90% of the value of the Dow at that time. A decline of nearly 500 points in the mid-1970s represented a much smaller percentage of the Dow's value.

average around 1884 for use in his *Customer's Afternoon Letter*. The first list of industrials was published in 1896 and was literally an average of the prices of 12 selected industrial stocks. For the sake of continuity, however, the formula has been revised to reflect *stock splits* and changes in the company composition of the overall stock market. (A stock split is a division of a company's outstanding shares so that a greater number of shares is created, each having a lower face value, so that the total value of the shares remains the same.)

The Dow provides a simple way to follow the course of the market as a whole. From 70.1 at the end of 1900, it described a jagged path between a low of 42.15 in 1903 and pre–World War I peaks of 103 and 100.53 in 1906 and 1909. For most of the next decade, the Dow continued to fluctuate cyclically within a range of 53.17 and 109.88. It began a steep and steady climb in 1921.

The 1920s marked the first time the general public participated significantly in the stock market. Investment money poured in and by 1929 the Dow had reached a giddy peak of 381.17. Overconfident investors had gone deep into debt to invest all that they could in the rapidly appreciating stocks. When the bubble burst, it did so catastrophically. The crash of 1929 eventually brought the Dow all the way down to 41.22 in 1932—the Dow's 20th-century low.

The establishment of the SEC in 1934 was part of Congress's attempt to cope with the excesses of the 1920s boom and the problems of the Great Depression that followed the stock-market crash of '29. Since then, the Dow has been on an erratic upward slope, surging with the rapid post–World War II industrial expansion to 995.15 in 1966. In early 1987, the Dow broke 2,000 for the first time. The significance attached to that purely psychological barrier and the euphoric press reaction that accompanied the breakthrough reflected the Dow's importance in the financial world.

The real significance of the Dow Jones industrial average is open to debate. It is now rather narrowly based on the prices of 30 of the largest companies in the nation, all of which are traded on the NYSE. It neglects the vast majority of stocks, which are too small or speculative for listing on the major exchanges. Also, the index's readings are highly sensitive to changes in its sample composition. If, for example, IBM had not been dropped from the list of companies used for the average in favor of AT&T in 1928, the Dow would be roughly twice what it is today. (While the stock value of both companies has grown phenomenally, that of IBM has outpaced that of AT&T.)

(continued from page 17)

To attract attention to the first stock issued by Nuclear Corporation of America, the vice-president of the company, Kennard Morganstern (left), and the president of the American Stock Exchange, Edward McCormick, demonstrate the company's product to Wall Street on October 10, 1955. They hold nuclear energy devices to activate the market's ticker keyboards, sending the latest stock and bond quotations throughout the United States and Canada.

Today, with the country's great wealth and industry's growing appetite for capital, the volume of shares traded on the NYSE, AMEX, and regional exchanges has multiplied many times since the early 1900s, more than tripling between 1974 and 1980. The NYSE is now the largest stock exchange in the world, and the AMEX the second largest in the United States.

The OTC has been strengthened by changes in trading regulations and an increasingly sophisticated computer and telecommunications network. Having been overshadowed by the other more formal, centralized exchanges for much of the stock market's history, the OTC has recently grown to rival them in importance. The market actually ranks second behind the NYSE in daily share volume.

The table on page 24 shows the trading activity of these stock markets during 1986. The actual number of shares traded was considerably higher because the figures do not include OTC stocks not listed on the National Association of Security Dealers Automatic Quotation system (NASDAQ).

At the end of a heavy day of trading, a market analyst tries to catch up on late stock market ticker-tape reports, May 28, 1962. Stocks declined sharply that day, and the ticker-tape machines could not keep up with the selling activity.

ISSUING AND TRADING STOCKS

Today, Wall Street provides two kinds of markets for the issuing and trading of securities: a *primary market* and a *secondary market*. The investment process begins with the primary market. When a company wants to expand its business, it can sell stocks and bonds to the public to raise capital. A company does this through the primary market. The process of bringing stocks to the market for the first time is called *going public*.

The Primary Market

In the primary market, the central figure is the *investment banker*, a person who specializes in raising the capital needed by businesses for long-term growth. A corporation's treasurer will work closely with an investment banker to raise funds.

Investment bankers are generally employed by large investment firms that perform a wide range of functions. They help companies raise capital by *underwriting* new issues of stocks and bonds and arranging for them to be sold to the investing public. The investment banker acts as a liaison between the company and Wall Street, guiding the company into the public marketplace and introducing investors to it.

Suppose that a private company (one that has never previously issued stock to the public) has enjoyed several years of success and now wants to expand. The company's management has determined that several million dollars are needed. The treasurer contacts an investment banker to explore alternatives for raising capital, including the possibility of going public.

In order to recommend an appropriate method of financing, the investment banker must consider many factors. These include general economic conditions, the Wall Street market environment at the time, and the company's particular situation, including its present financial condition, its history of earnings, and business prospects over the next several years for the company and its industry group. These and other factors will also be used later to establish an offering price for the stock, should the investment banker decide that a stock issue is the company's best avenue and that his or her bank will underwrite it.

A new computer system for branch offices of investment firms was introduced in September 1982. The Intellimation system (right) could support 10 stock quotation terminals (left) and serve investors by projecting market trends graphically and updating the value of their stock portfolios.

ISSUING
AND TRADING

23

MARKET ACTIVITY, 1986

MARKET	SHARES TRADED	DOLLAR VALUE
	(in thousands)	*(in millions)*
New York Stock Exchange	35,680,016	1,374,350
OTC (NASDAQ)	28,736,551	378,216
American Stock Exchange	2,978,612	43,649

In this case, the investment banker decides that a public offering of stock would be appropriate to raise capital, as opposed to a form of debt obligation such as issuing bonds. Seeing that the company has bright prospects for the future, the investment banker's firm agrees to underwrite the issue. A group of investment bankers, in conjunction with the firm's research analysts and traders, determines a price for a single share of stock. The price should be attractive to investors who are likely to purchase the stock. To underwrite the issue, the investment bankers then buy all of the available shares of stock from the company for resale to the public. It is thereafter up to the investment banking firm to resell the shares of stock to individual and institutional investors around the country. If the offering price is attractive to investors, this should not be difficult.

Before a new issue can be sold, however, the company must comply with the full disclosure requirements of the SEC, which closely watches over all new offerings of stock. The company has to list the essential facts of its financial condition, including five years of detailed, audited financial history and a complete description of the business, in registration statements filed with the SEC. These facts are also printed in a *prospectus*, which investment bankers must give to every potential buyer at the time they are considering whether to buy the stock. This is to ensure that every investor knows what he or she is buying. The prospectus must explain how the company intends to use the capital from stock sales.

If a large number of shares are being issued, it is possible that not all of the stock will be sold. This risk can be shared by inviting other investment bankers to join in an underwriting group called a *syndicate*. At the time of a sale, the syndicate members usually invite other securities dealers to join them to help sell the new shares to the public. The shares will be sold at a set price by everyone in the syndicate. In general, this is the only time a stock price is ever fixed—when the price is temporarily supported by the underwriters. After that, the shares are traded as usual according to the laws of *supply and demand*. This type of transaction takes place in the secondary market.

The Secondary Market

The secondary market is, like the primary market, not an actual place. It is a loose term used to describe the cumulative buying and selling of the stocks of more than 24,000 publicly traded companies that have already issued shares. It is composed of nine different stock exchanges located around the country and the vast over-the-counter

A Long Island Railroad Company stock certificate representing ownership of 60,000 shares of the company's stock. Companies raise money for expansion and operations by issuing, or selling, stock to the public.

The trading floor of the New York Stock Exchange in 1978. Stock exchanges and the OTC market are the secondary market in which stocks are sold to the public.

(OTC) stock market, which consists of a network of *broker/dealers* who buy and sell stocks through a sophisticated computer system. The secondary market provides investors with an adequate number of bids to buy and offers to sell particular stocks, as well as a place to sell shares at any time. Without the secondary market, investors would have no organized, efficient system for locating stocks, finding out their prices, and buying (or selling) them.

In the same way that a corporate treasurer works closely with an investment banker in the primary market, the investor's main contact in the secondary market is the *account executive (AE)* or *stockbroker*, technically referred to as a registered representative because he or she is registered with the SEC and represents the customer or client.

Account executives generally are affiliated with large brokerage firms that may have thousands of AEs working at dozens of branch offices around the country. The AE does not actually buy from or sell to the customer, but rather acts on the customer's behalf as an agent. The brokerage firm receives a commission on every transaction, a percentage of which goes to the AE.

Prior to May 1, 1975, this commission was fixed according to the number of shares involved in the trade and their price. When this system was abandoned, it ended a practice that had begun in 1792, when the first members of the NYSE agreed to charge fixed rates. Now commissions on all orders are negotiated, enabling an investor to bargain with brokers for the lowest rate. Of course, major financial institutions, such as pension funds, banks, insurance companies, and mutual funds, all of which trade stocks in large amounts called *blocks*, have the greatest bargaining power. Sometimes they involve millions of dollars in a single order. A lower percentage commission on each institutional trade still amounts to a great deal of money.

Since the passage of the 1975 law, a new type of brokerage firm, known as a *discount broker*, has sprung up. Discount brokers have flourished by executing stock transactions for extremely low commission rates. They are able to charge low rates primarily because they offer only the service of buying and selling stock for a customer; they do not give advice on stocks.

Brokerage Firms

The brokerage firms that facilitate the buying and selling of stocks in the secondary market offer various services. The main office of a large NYSE member firm, for example, usually has trading departments for the stocks listed on the various exchanges, OTC stocks, and various types of bonds;

a research department where securities analysts appraise for the investor the investment potential of specific stocks and investment strategies; an underwriting department that gathers buyers for new stock issues; and a corporate finance department for planning company financing. In addition the main office will have an operations department that keeps records, handles payments, and safely stores stock certificates and other documents. Smaller firms may offer only a few of these services. Some specialize solely in the execution of orders. All investment firms, however, must conform to extensive SEC requirements as well as additional exchange or OTC rules, which are all intended to protect investors.

Major brokerages have membership in one or more stock exchanges. Only a firm that is a member of a particular stock exchange is allowed to execute orders on the trading floor of that exchange. To become a member, a brokerage firm must buy a *seat*, an expression that recalls the days when brokers were seated during stock auctions. Because the number of seats is limited, they are sold, like stocks, in their own auction market. In early 1987, a seat on the NYSE was sold for one million dollars, breaking all previous records.

Firms that do not own seats are called *nonmember firms*. Their orders for exchange-listed stocks must be executed by a representative of a member firm.

A brokerage firm that does most of its commission business with individual investors is referred to as a *retail house*. Other firms, known as *institutional houses*, obtain most of their commission income by assisting large *institutional investors* such as mutual funds, pension funds, insurance companies, and banks. These investors put hundreds of millions of dollars into the stock market and can generate large commissions for their brokers. Many brokerages, of course, are able to handle both retail and institutional business.

Account executives (stockbrokers) at work in New York City.

THE STOCK EXCHANGES

The nine current stock exchanges in the United States are the NYSE, AMEX, Boston Stock Exchange, Cincinnati Stock Exchange, Intermountain Stock Exchange, Midwest Stock Exchange, Pacific Stock Exchange, Philadelphia Stock Exchange, and Spokane Stock Exchange. Of these, the largest and best known are the first two. The others are considered regional exchanges. The existence of the regional exchanges increases the overall *liquidity* (the ability of the market in a particular stock to absorb a great volume of trading without major price fluctuation) of the marketplace and gives companies more choices and flexibility when they want to list a stock.

Today the five larger regional exchanges (Pacific, Midwest, Philadelphia, Boston, and Cincinnati) are linked by a computer system with the New York and American exchanges. This has led to a truly national listing for many stocks.

Listing a Stock

Entrance to the New York Stock Exchange, the largest stock exchange in the world.

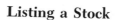

When a stock is *listed* on one of the exchanges, it has been accepted for trading there. The term has been retained from the time when the daily list of stocks was read to the assembled brokers at auctions more than a century ago. Before its stock can be listed, a company must meet certain minimum requirements.

Each exchange has its own minimums. For a company to be among the more than 2,200 on the NYSE, for example, it must meet a combination of requirements such as having pretax earnings of $2.5 million in the latest year; a total of 1.1 million shares publicly held; and at least 2,000 holders of 100–share lots of its stock. The OTC has less stringent minimum requirements, making it easier for smaller companies to be listed there. A company can eventually be "delisted" if it

(continued on page 34)

Where the Stock Exchanges Are

New York City is where the action is, but there are stock exchanges around the world, as well as elsewhere in the United States. Chicago has the Midwest Exchange, San Francisco has the Pacific Exchange, and other important exchanges are located in Philadelphia and Boston. Elsewhere in North America there are major exchanges in Toronto, Montreal, and Mexico City. South America has an exchange in Buenos Aires, Argentina.

Europe's major exchanges are in London, Paris, Brussels, Frankfurt, Zurich, Amsterdam, and Milan, with smaller ones in Vienna, Oslo, Copenhagen, and Madrid. Across the Pacific Ocean, there are important exchanges in Tokyo, Hong Kong, Singapore, and Sydney. The local currency is always used wherever stocks are traded—Canadian dollars, Japanese yen, Mexican pesos, Swiss francs.

The Tokyo Stock Exchange trades more shares than any other in the world, and it is second only to New York in dollar value. The huge volume is due largely to low prices per share of stock; investors get more shares for their money. Japan is so highly computerized that virtually no real stock certificates change hands; everything is held in computer memory.

The London Stock Exchange ranks behind those of New York and Tokyo in

American floor traders from Merrill Lynch watch Japanese hand signals on their first day of trading in Tokyo. In February 1986, the firm became the first foreign securities company to trade on the Tokyo Stock Exchange.

dollar value of trading but stands first in the number of companies listed. About half of all stocks on the London exchange are foreign. Bonds are listed in addition to stocks, which accounts for the large number of listings. In England the language of investments is somewhat different from American terminology. What we call common stocks are known there as ordinary shares, while British government bonds are "gilt-edged" stocks, or "gilts."

At the other extreme is the small but active Bolsa de Valores in Mexico City, with fewer than 100 companies listed. The stocks of about 75 companies are traded in Mexico on an average day. Daily volume is about 50 million shares. There are only about 200,000 regular investors, but interest in investing is growing so quickly that some brokers are opening as many as 100 new accounts every day.

Brokers on the Bourse, as the Paris exchange is called, are known as *agents de change*. All of them belong to the association that regulates the investment industry through its own annually elected governing board, the Chambre Syndicale. The exchange itself is divided into three sections, which correspond roughly to the NYSE, AMEX, and OTC, respectively, in the types of companies that they attract.

The major Canadian market is the Toronto Stock Exchange. The less active Montreal exchange, however, is more prestigious, being the primary market for several blue-chip companies. The smaller Vancouver Stock Exchange primarily trades stocks of oil and mineral exploration companies. Calgary also has its own exchange.

The world's newest stock exchanges are also its smallest, although they are located in its most populous nation: China. The Beijing exchange lists one stock; Shanghai's has four stocks and two

(left) Customers line up on August 12, 1986, to purchase bonds on the first day of trading at the Shenyang Exchange. (right) Agents de change on the floor of the Bourse watch stock prices and shout orders.

Capitalization* of Major World Stock Exchanges

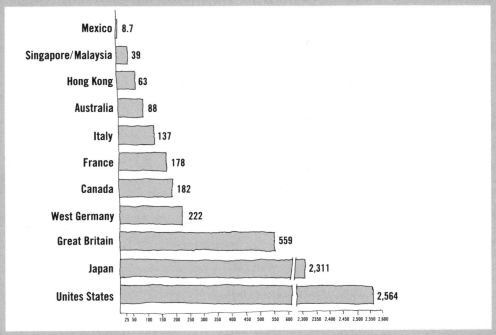

Mexico	8.7
Singapore/Malaysia	39
Hong Kong	63
Australia	88
Italy	137
France	178
Canada	182
West Germany	222
Great Britain	559
Japan	2,311
Unites States	2,564

25 50 100 150 200 250 300 350 400 450 500 550 600 2,300 2350 2,400 2,450 2,500 2,550 2,600

*in billions of U.S. dollars, as of February 27, 1987.   Source: *New York Times*, March 30, 1987.

bonds. When one of the bond issues went on sale for the first time in January of 1987, 3,000 people lined up, many waiting overnight to place their orders.

The market in Shanghai was once the largest in Asia, but following the Revolution of 1949, all stock exchanges in China were closed. In August 1986 the Shenyang exchange in northern China became the first to reopen, followed within months by four other markets. The Beijing exchange is open only on Tuesday and Friday mornings and has little activity. In Shanghai, trading takes place every day, although people may have to wait a few weeks before they can buy the stock they want. Throughout China, there are more prospective buyers than sellers of shares of stocks or bonds. Few people want to sell because prices are fixed by market officials and are not allowed to rise in response to the demands of interested buyers. In China, unlike other world markets, foreigners are not allowed to trade on the Chinese stock exchanges.

(continued from page 30)

falls below these requirements. The net effect of the various listing requirements has been to attract the oldest, largest, and best-known companies to the NYSE; smaller and younger companies to the AMEX; and the youngest, least-experienced companies to the OTC market. There are some important exceptions to this generalization. Several large, well-known companies such as Betz Laboratories, McCormick & Co., Noxell Corporation, Yellow Freight, and others have not sought NYSE listing by their own choice. Among other things, they prefer the multiple-trading that is possible through a variety of broker/dealers.

A company can be listed on more than one exchange. The advantage to this is a broader exposure in the stock market to investors. Dual listings are common on the regional exchanges. A company will usually be listed on one

The trading floor of the American Stock Exchange, 1971. The hand signals of curbstone brokers are still used by floor brokers and clerks to communicate price and order information.

of the New York exchanges in addition to a regional exchange. Because of the higher volume of trading in the New York markets, the transactions in dually traded stocks are usually based on current NYSE or AMEX prices. However, most companies listed on the regional exchanges are local or regional businesses.

TRADING SHARES OF STOCK

How does Wall Street's system of trading stocks work for an investor? First, the investor opens an account with a brokerage firm, which is in many ways similar to opening a bank account. Once this is done, the investor can buy or sell stocks through any exchange or the OTC, with his or her stockbroker acting as the agent. To understand how the trading system works, consider this example of two people, one of whom is buying and the other selling a stock listed on the NYSE.

A store owner in Atlanta, Georgia, telephones her account executive at a local branch of a NYSE brokerage firm and gives a *market order* to buy 100 shares (the standard unit of trading, commonly called a *round lot*) of the XYZ Company. A market order is an order to be carried out as soon as possible at the best price available.

At about the same time, a teacher in Denver, Colorado, places a market order with his local broker, also at a firm that is a member of the NYSE, to sell 100 shares of XYZ Company stock. The orders are quickly sent to the trading departments of the respective firms and then transmitted directly to the floor of the NYSE. The firms' *floor brokers* (employees located on the trading floor of the exchange) receive the orders from one of several teletype machines serving the trading area.

The New York Stock Exchange, April 1978. Stock trading can seem complex to many people.

Once the floor brokers have the orders, they proceed to the *trading post* where XYZ stock is bought and sold. Every listed stock is traded at one of several specific locations on the floor. Like all listed stocks, the XYZ Company stock has a *specialist* assigned to it. The specialist's primary function is to keep trade in that stock fair and orderly. To do this, the specialist maintains an account for the stock, buying shares for that account when supply outstrips demand, and selling when there are too many buyers and not enough sellers. Without a specialist, a company's stock prices might fluctuate erratically—sellers might not be able to sell and buyers might not be able to buy.

At the post where XYZ is traded, the brokers enter the *crowd*, which is a group of two or more brokers who also have orders for XYZ. "How's XYZ?" asks the broker representing the Atlanta store owner. "Thirty and three eighths to three quarters," someone responds. This is the current *bid-and-asked quotation*. This means that 30⅜ ($30.375) is the best bid, the most anyone in the crowd is then willing to pay; and 30¾ ($30.75) is the best offer, the lowest price at which anyone will sell. The difference between the bid and asked prices is called the *spread*.

The store owner's broker tries to get a better price than the offer by saying "thirty and one half for one hundred." If there is no response, the broker will raise the bid in increments of ⅛ of a dollar (12½ cents), which is the minimum unit of change for most stocks. Perhaps at 30⅝ ($30.625) the teacher's broker, feeling that it is the best price he can expect to get at that time, shouts "Sold!" This ends the transaction.

Once the orders are executed for the two customers,

their respective brokers notify them of the trade. This can happen within minutes after the order was first sent to the floor. The XYZ Company's stock symbol and the execution price of the trade are both printed immediately on the consolidated ticker tape on the trading floor, which is displayed electronically in brokerage offices throughout the country.

Floor brokers working at the New York Stock Exchange, 1985.

TRADING
SHARES

The Role of the Specialist

If there had been no offers to sell XYZ stock when the floor broker representing the Atlanta customer arrived at the trading post, the purchase could still have been made. The floor broker would have been able to buy stock for the store owner from the specialist's own account. Similarly, if there had been no offers to buy XYZ stock when the floor broker representing the Denver client arrived at the trading post, the sale could still have been made. The floor broker would have been able to sell stock to the specialist's account.

A specialist maintains an account for several different companies' stocks. Specialists keep a separate inventory of the buy and sell orders for each of their assigned stocks in what is called a specialist's book. The specialist's book contains orders that cannot be executed immediately because they are "away from the market." That is, the orders to sell are at a price higher than the price at which the stock is currently being traded, and orders to buy are at a lower price. The specialist, or the specialist's firm, must always have enough capital on hand to buy 5,000 shares of any assigned stock. In order to uphold the commitment to preserve a fair and orderly market, the specialist attempts to keep the spread between the price to buy a stock and the price to sell it narrow and to minimize any sharp price fluctuations.

When specialists trade for their own accounts, they are said to be acting as *dealers*, much like the dealers in the OTC market. A dealer acts as a *principal* in a transaction, buying from and selling stock to a customer. A broker, on the other hand, only represents a customer, acting as an intermediary or agent.

A trade of fewer than 100 shares of a stock is known as an *odd lot*. If an investor wants to buy or sell an odd lot, the specialist also acts as a dealer. On the NYSE, an odd-lot order, processed by computer, is automatically executed at the next round-lot price struck at the trading post. The specialist receives periodic reports of how many odd-lot shares have been added to or subtracted from the inventory in each stock's account. For serving as a dealer in odd-lot trades, the specialist usually charges the customer an additional 1/8 point (12½ cents) per share, called the odd-lot differential or the odd-lot premium.

Trading in the OTC Market

If the Atlanta store owner had wanted to buy 100 shares of an OTC stock rather than the NYSE-listed stock, her order would have been sent to the brokerage firm's OTC trading desk rather than to the regular trading desk and then to an exchange floor. This is because OTC stocks are not traded in a central exchange. The individuals at the OTC desk in the brokerage house are referred to as *broker/dealers* because they can act in either capacity, depending on the circumstances.

If the firm's broker/dealer *makes a market* in that particular stock, the store owner's order may be filled directly from the firm's inventory. A broker/dealer makes a market by maintaining an inventory of the stock. A dealer must be willing to trade it at any time; be prepared to buy or sell at least 100 shares at any point; and announce bid-and-asked prices continuously. In this situation, the broker/dealer acts as a principal, or dealer, and is known as a market maker for that stock. These rules for making a market are necessary to keep prices and trading in the OTC market fair because there is no formal, supervised auction process comparable to that of an exchange.

The OTC trading department at a brokerage, through the broker/dealer, quotes a single price, which includes the commission, to the customer. The customer may try to negotiate for a lower price. As soon as the customer and the dealer agree, the order is completed.

The customer may desire a stock in which the broker/dealer does not make a market. Because most OTC stock prices are quoted in the NASDAQ system, the broker/dealer calls up the company on the system's computer. The dealer's terminal, which consists of a keyboard and a screen or monitor, is tied electronically to the system's main computer. Typing the trading symbol of the stock on the keyboard brings the current bid-and-asked quotations of that stock instantly onto the screen. The quotations are from the dealers who do make a market in that stock and their names are listed with their quotations. There may be 10 or more market makers for a given stock.

The broker/dealer then calls the market maker who is offering the best quotation, negotiates a price, and buys the stock for the customer. In this transaction, the broker/dealer has acted as a broker or agent and charges the customer a commission.

If the stock is not among the nearly 5,000 currently being quoted on NASDAQ, the broker/dealer will have to locate a dealer who is a market maker in the stock to negotiate a price directly. Market makers are listed in the *pink sheets*. The pink sheets are a roster of all OTC market makers and their latest price quotations, published daily by the National Quotation Service. Finding a market maker for a stock in this way may take longer but is otherwise identical to a NASDAQ-system trade.

An investor studies stock quotations at a New York brokerage firm branch office.

INDIVIDUAL AND INSTITUTIONAL INVESTORS

Shares of stocks can be bought and owned by two kinds of investors: single individuals and institutions. A 1984 NYSE survey of investors calculated that there were 42 million individual shareholders. Although stockholder characteristics vary considerably, the survey found that the average shareowner was 44.5 years old, female, had an annual household income of $33,200, and held a portfolio of stocks worth $5,100.

Individual shareholders used to own the largest portion of all issued stocks. In recent years, however, institutional investors have steadily replaced individuals as the dominant force in the stock market. The largest institutional investors are noninsured pension funds, investment companies, not-for-profit organizations, insurance companies, common trust funds, and savings banks. Today, institutional investors hold roughly one third of the $1 trillion total market value for all NYSE-listed stocks. If the shares owned by foreign institutions, private funds, and certain other funds were included, total institutional holdings might represent as much as half of the value of all NYSE stocks.

The main difference between institutional and individual investors is in the size of their stock portfolios and the dollar value of their transactions. While a very wealthy individual may have several million dollars in investments, large institutional investors may buy and sell stocks worth that amount in a single afternoon. Recently, the number and influence of large institutional investors have grown immensely. With a single multimillion-dollar stock trade, an institutional investor can cause a dramatic swing in a stock's price.

RECENT TRENDS AND A LOOK TOWARD THE FUTURE

In the last 25 years computers have greatly affected the overall functioning of the stock market. Breakthroughs in computer and communications technology have sped up the process of buying and selling large quantities of stock. New equipment, recently installed, makes it possible for the NYSE to trade more than 200 million shares of stock a day. But 30 years ago, 50–million-share days would have been more than the technology of the time could handle promptly. Before computers arrived, trading frequently had to be halted until the ticker tape machines on which transactions were recorded caught up with the trading activity on the floor.

Computers make it possible to register hundreds of buy or sell orders at the same time. They can also gather orders from various investment firms into large blocks to make them easier to handle and remind specialists of standing orders to buy or sell a stock when it reaches a certain price. Computer programs to consolidate trading activity on the various exchanges are now in place. By combining data from separate markets, these programs attempt to expose each order to the best bid-and-asked prices no matter where they occur, which ultimately leads to a more efficient system for trading.

One of the newest developments in the U.S. stock market is nighttime

The computer room of the New York Stock Exchange in the late 1970s.

trading. The Chicago Board of Trade was the first to initiate such extended hours in April 1987 for specialized bond trading. This makes it possible for investors in Asia to trade with Chicago on the same day. This is just the beginning for this concept. If all of the exchanges in the U.S. extend their hours to tie in with the times when Asian and European markets are open, a truly international investment market is possible. With the use of more advanced computer systems, computers could link stock exchanges around the world, and investors could trade 24 hours a day.

Spectators toss ticker tape from windows along Broadway to honor astronaut Gordon Cooper on May 22, 1963. A ticker-tape parade honoring headline-making heroes has long been a Wall Street area tradition.

GLOSSARY

account executive (AE), stockbroker, broker An agent who acts as an intermediary between buyers and sellers of securities.

American Stock Exchange (AMEX) One of the major U.S. stock markets, located in New York City; originally called the Curb.

bear market A market in which stock prices are consistently falling. *See* bull market.

bid-and-asked quotation The constantly changing prices involved in the trading of stocks. In a stock auction, the highest price someone is willing to pay for a stock at a given time (bid), in combination with the lowest price at which someone will sell (asked).

block A grouping of 10,000 or more shares of stock.

bond A certificate that represents a loan to a company or government agency. The issuing company (the borrower) pays interest for the use of the money and must repay the entire amount of the bond at a specified time.

broker/dealer A person who acts in the capacity of broker or dealer, depending on the circumstances of a stock transaction. Broker/dealers work primarily in the OTC market. *See also* account executive.

brokerage, brokerage firm, or **investment firm** An organization that represents customers in buying and selling stocks and other types of investments.

bull market A market in which stock prices are consistently rising. *See* bear market.

commission A fee paid to an agent for a business transaction. It is usually figured as a percentage of the dollar value of the transaction.

dealer A person (or brokerage firm) that maintains an inventory of stocks and buys or sells them as a principal rather than on behalf of an individual.

discount broker A type of brokerage firm that handles only the transactions of buying and selling stocks for customers.

floor broker A person employed by a brokerage who carries out orders on the floor of a stock exchange to buy and sell stocks.

going public A company's sale of shares of its stock to the public for the first time.

institutional house A brokerage that transacts most of its commission business with large institutional investors. *See* retail house.

institutional investor An organization such as an insurance company or pension fund that invests large amounts of money in securities.

investment banker A person who arranges company financing through the issue of new stocks and bonds.

investment banking firm An organization that helps companies raise money by underwriting new stock and bond issues.

issue The offer of a company's securities for sale; the sale of a company's securities. Also, the actual shares being sold.

liquidity The ease with which an investor can sell stock.

listed Status of a company whose stock has been accepted for trading on a particular exchange.

make a market To be a dealer in a particular OTC stock, holding a quantity of that stock for sale to investors.

market order An order to buy or sell a security as soon as possible at the best obtainable price.

NASDAQ (pronounced "nazdak") The computerized National Association of Securities Dealers Automatic Quotation network that provides price quotations on stocks and bonds traded over-the-counter.

New York Stock Exchange (NYSE) The major U.S. market where shares of stock are traded; originally called the New York Stock and Exchange Board.

odd lot Any number of shares of stock less than the established 100-share unit. *See* round lot.

over-the-counter (OTC) market The nationwide network of brokers who handle transactions of stocks that are not listed on an exchange.

pink sheets A daily list of OTC stocks not traded on NASDAQ that includes the names of the broker/dealers making a market in them and the price quotations of the previous day.

primary market Trading of newly issued stocks.

principals The customers for whom a broker buys or sells stock, or traders who buy or sell for their own accounts.

prospectus The official public report of a company that must be given to potential buyers of a newly issued stock.

retail house A brokerage firm that does most of its commission business with individual investors. *See* institutional house.

round lot A standard unit of trading for a security. For stocks, 100 shares. *See* odd lot.

seat Membership on a stock exchange. Required for a brokerage or an individual to execute stock orders on that exchange.

secondary market Trading of stocks that have already been issued.

securities Stock certificates or bonds that are evidence of property or debt.

Securities and Exchange Commission (SEC) A U.S. government agency established by Congress in 1934 to regulate the trading of stocks and bonds to protect investors.

share of stock Any of the equal parts into which the entire value of a company is divided. It represents part ownership in the company.

specialist A stockbroker who handles specific stocks on the floor of a stock exchange. The specialist seeks to maintain a fair and orderly market for the stocks to which he or she is assigned.

spread The numerical difference between the bid and asked prices of a stock.

stock split The division of a company's outstanding shares of stock so that a greater number of shares is created, each having lower face value, so that the total value of the shares remains the same.

supply and demand The relationship between the price, quantity available, and demand for an item or service, including shares of stock. When demand is high and supply is low, people are willing to pay more.

syndicate A group of investment bankers who join together to share the risk of underwriting and distributing a new stock issue.

trading post A numbered location on an exchange floor where specific company stocks are traded.

underwriting The process of buying newly issued securities from a corporation and reselling them to the public. Investment banking firms underwrite new issues.

FURTHER READING

Most daily newspapers carry financial news of interest to investors, along with stock quotation tables. Major papers such as the *New York Times* and the *Washington Post* contain extensive sections of business and financial news on weekdays and Sundays.

Rosenberg, Claude N., Jr. *Stock Market Primer*. New York: World, 1969. Provides the first-time investor with a clear introduction to the workings of the stock market.

Sobel, Robert. *Inside Wall Street*. New York: Norton, 1977. A history of Wall Street and such financial institutions as the NYSE and AMEX.

Teweles, Richard J., and Edward S. Bradley. *The Stock Market*. 4th rev. ed. New York: Wiley, 1982. An overview of the stock market, including a discussion of domestic and foreign stock exchanges; contains an extensive glossary.

Wall Street Journal. The newspaper of the business world; provides a wide range of financial news, including updates on corporations; published weekdays.

And a resource: New York Stock Exchange, Visitor's Center, 20 Broad Street, 3d floor, New York, New York. Permanent exhibits; free tour includes gallery viewing of the trading floor. Advance reservations necessary for groups of more than 10.

INDEX

JEFFREY B. LITTLE, a finance graduate of New York University, began his Wall Street career in the early 1960s. He has worked as an accountant for a retail brokerage firm, as an instructor of technical analysis in a broker training center, as a securities analyst of technology stocks, and as a portfolio manager and advisory committee member for a major mutual fund. He is a Fellow of the Financial Analysts Federation, a member of the New York Society of Security Analysts, and was formerly a vice-president of an investment counsel firm in Baltimore.

PAUL A. SAMUELSON, senior editorial consultant, is Institute Professor Emeritus at the Massachusetts Institute of Technology. He is author (now coauthor) of the best-selling textbook *Economics.* He served as an adviser to President John F. Kennedy and in 1970 was the first American to win the Nobel Prize in economics.

SHAWN PATRICK BURKE, consulting editor, is a securities analyst with Standard & Poor's Corporation. He has been an internal consultant in industry as well as for a Wall Street investment firm, and he has extensive experience in computer-generated financial modeling and analysis.

ROBERT W. WRUBEL, contributing editor, is an associate editor with *Financial World* magazine and was previously associate financial editor with Boardroom Reports, Inc. A graduate of Yale University, he has been a financial analyst for a Wall Street securities firm and has written extensively on finance and investment topics.